# Let's enjoy Japanese!
# 日本語 を 楽しもう！
nihongo　o　tanoshimō !

### The Japanese unique expressions
### which are inimitable for foreign languages

**Nobuko Ishida  &  Tamao Uchida**

Seiga shobō

# PREFACE

The Japanese language has a unique and interesting way of expressing a situation by doubling a word. At the point of doubling a word, it is similar to an onomatopoeic word. The onomatopoeia expresses cries of animals like quack-quack for a duck or moo-moo for a cow, but this doubling word in Japanese expresses a situation of the mind, the body and things, etc. Also, it expresses a movement of people, animals and plants, etc. I do not know the exact word in English to explain this interesting expression. However, if you once learn to use this expression, you will enjoy speaking Japanese more than you used to.

There are many more examples than I have introduced here. This time I just picked out some of them to introduce you to the unique and interesting Japanese language.

I hope this book will be your good friend and will be the beginning of making the Japanese language more interesting and enjoyable.

I want to express my appreciation to Mrs. Michael R. Cox, Nancy, who helped me with the English part. Nancy is my long time American friend. We have been good friends since 1958.

I also want to express my appreciation to Mr. Tamao Uchida who drew all the pictures in this book. These pictures will help you to understand   each situation at a glance. He is a professional cartoonist and is the husband of my Japanese good friend, Kazuko.

I am very grateful to Mr. Fuminori Sekine who had an interest in and actuated the publishing of this book. He is the president of SEIGA SHOBŌ.

I also appreciate the International Business Division of KINOKUNIYA SHOTEN (KINOKUNIYA COMPANY LTD.) which obligingly complied with my request to introduce this book in many foreign countries.

And finally, I want to give my hearty thanks to my husband, Yuji, who helped me greatly by pleasantly following my earnest request to arrange and type the draft of this book.

With a hope for your enjoyment,<br>
Nobuko Ishida

# Contents

Preface　2

フーフー　hū hū　4
フーフー　hū hū　5
クンクン　kun kun　6
ポタポタ　pota pota　7
シクシク　shiku shiku　8
ワーワー　wā wā　9
メソメソ　meso meso　10
クヨクヨ　kuyo kuyo　11
ピョンピョン　pyon pyon　12
ゾロゾロ　zoro zoro　13
シャナリシャナリ
　　shanari shanari　14
ヨチヨチ　yochi yochi　15
ソロソロ　soro soro　16
ピチャピチャ　picha picha　17
トボトボ　tobo tobo　18
テクテク　teku teku　19
ドンドン　don don　20
ドンドン　don don　21
ザーザー　zā zā　22
シトシト　shito shito　23
ポツポツ　potsu potsu　24
ブカブカ　buka buka　25
ベトベト　beto beto　26
ベトベト　beto beto　27
チクチク　chiku chiku　28
ヒリヒリ　hiri hiri　29
シクシク　shiku shiku　30
サクサク　saku saku　31
ジャンジャン　jyan jyan　32
フサフサ　husa husa　33
ユラユラ　yura yura　34

ユラユラ　yura yura　35
クルクル　kuru kuru　36
サンサン　san san　37
キラキラ　kira kira　38
ミチミチ　コツコツ
　　michi michi　kotsu kotsu　39
ヒラヒラ　ハラハラ
　　hira hira　hara hara　40
ハラハラ　ドキドキ
　　hara hara　doki doki　41
ドキドキ　doki doki　42
ワクワク　waku waku　43
ルンルン　run run　44
ニコニコ　niko niko　45
オロオロ　oro oro　46
ボロボロ　boro boro　47
ボロボロ　boro boro　48
モヤモヤ　moya moya　49
ゾクゾク　zoku zoku　50
ゾクゾク　zoku zoku　51
ジロジロ　jiro jiro　52
キョロキョロ　kyoro kyoro　53
スクスク　suku suku　54
コロコロ　koro koro　55
ゴシゴシ　goshi goshi　56
ユサユサ　yusa yusa　57
イライラ　ira ira　58
ツルツル　tsuru tsuru　59
ギュウギュウ　gyū gyū　60
ヒソヒソ　hiso hiso　61
ガヤガヤ　gaya gaya　62
ペラペラ　pera pera　63

熱い お茶 を フーフー する。
atsui ocha o hū hū suru.

*Blow on the hot tea to cool it off.*

仕事　が　いっぱい で　フーフー
shigoto　ga　ippai　　　de　hū hū

言っちゃう。
　icchau.


*I have just too much work to get done.*

犬 が 食べ物　の においを
inu ga tabemono no nioi　o

**クンクン** かいでいます。
**kun kun** kaideimasu.

*A dog is sniffing the food.*

水　が　ポタポタ　垂れています。
mizu ga　　pota pota　tareteimasu.

*Water is dripping one drop at a time.*

女の子　が　シクシク
on-nanoko ga　shiku shiku

泣いています。
naiteimasu.

*A girl is crying softly.*

男の子　が　ワーワー
otokonoko ga　wā　wā

泣いています。
naiteimasu.

*A boy is crying very loudly.*

そんな事 で　メソメソ するな！
son-nakoto de　**meso meso**　suruna !

*Don't let that get your spirit down.*

クヨクヨ　して　何になるっ！
kuyo kuyo   shite   nan-ninaru !

*Worrying won't help you.*

うさぎ が ピョンピョン
usagi ga pyon pyon

跳ねている。
haneteiru.

*A rabbit is hopping.*

蟻が　ゾロゾロ　はっている。
ari ga　**zoro zoro**　hatteiru.

*Ants are crawling a long single file line.*

着物姿　　の　ご婦人 が
kimonosugata no　gohujin ga

シャナリシャナリ　と　歩いています。
shanari　shanari　to　aruiteimasu.

*A lady in Kimono walks very gracefully.*

赤ちゃん が ヨチ ヨチ 歩く。
akachan ga **yochi yochi** aruku.

*A baby takes one step at a time.*

お年寄り　の　女性　が
otoshiyori　no　jyosei ga

ソロソロ　歩いています。
**soro soro**　aruiteimasu.

*An old lady is walking carefully.*

子供　が　水たまり　を
kodomo ga　mizutamari o

ピチャピチャ　歩く。
**picha　picha**　aruku.

*A child splashes in the puddle as he walks along.*

悲しみ　で　トボトボ　歩く。
kanashimi de　tobo tobo　aruku.

*Walking with a down cast spirit.*

長道を テクテク 歩く。

nagamichi o **teku teku** aruku.

*Taking a long hike.*

若者 が ドンドン 歩く。
wakamono ga  don don  aruku.

*A young man walks very fast.*

仕事 が **ドンドン** 来る。

shigoto ga **don don** kuru.

*The work just keeps piling up.*

雨 が ザーザー 降る。
ame ga　zā　zā　　huru.

*It's raining cats and dogs.*

雨　が　シトシト　降っている。
ame　ga　shito shito　hutteiru.

*The rain is a gentle mist.*

雨 が ポツ ポツ 降っている。
ame ga  potsu potsu  hutteiru.

*The rain is dripping.*

この 洋服　は 私　　には
kono yōhuku wa　watashi niwa

ブカブカ　　だわ。
buka buka　　dawa.

*This dress is too big for me.*

飴　が　溶けて
ame ga　toke te

ベトベト　している。
**beto beto**　shiteiru.

*Candies are melted and are sticky.*

運動 を 楽しんだ　後 は、
undō　o　tanoshinda　ato wa

身体中　が 汗　で　ベトベト です。
karadajyū ga　ase　de　**beto beto**　desu.

*After enjoying sports, the body is very sweaty and sticky.*

私は　お腹が　チクチク
wtashi wa　onaka ga　chiku chiku

痛いです。
itaidesu.

*I have a sharp pain in my stomach.*

傷 が ヒリヒリ する。
kizu ga  hiri hiri  suru.

*The injury is very sore.*

女の子　の　虫歯　が
on-nanoko no　mushiba ga

シク シク　痛んでいます。
**shiku shiku**　itandeimasu.

*A girl has a toothache in her decayed tooth.*

この　クッキー　は
kono　kukki　　wa

サク サク　している。
**saku saku**　siteiru.

*This cookie is crispy.*

お金　を　ジャンジャン　使う。
okane　o　**jyan jyan**　tsukau.

*Spending money hand over fist.*

フサフサ　　した　髪の毛。
**husa husa**　　shita　kaminoke.

*A lot of hair.*

花々　　が　そよ風　で
hanabana ga　soyokaze de

ユラユラ　揺れている。
**yura yura**　yureteiru.

*Flowers sway in the breeze.*

ローソクの 炎 が
rōsoku no hono-o ga

**ユラユラ** 揺れている。
**yura yura** yureteiru.

*The candle flame flickers.*

踊り子 が　クルクル　回っている。
odoriko ga　**kuru kuru**　mawatteiru.

*A dancer is twirling round and round.*

太陽 が **サンサン** と 輝いている。
taiyō ga **san san** to kagayaiteiru.

*The sun is brightly shining.*

星 が キラキラ 輝いている。
hoshi ga kira kira kagayaiteiru.

*Stars are twinkling.*

彼 は ミチ ミチ コツ コツ
kare wa　michi michi　kotsu kotsu

勉強 を している。
benkyō o　shiteiru.

*He studies constantly and consistently.*

木の葉 が　ヒラヒラ　ハラ ハラ
konoha ga　　hira hira　　hara hara

舞い落ちる。
maiochiru.

*Leaves are dancing down one after another like feathers.*

受験生　が　入試　発表　を
jyukensei ga　nyushi　happyō　o

ハラハラ　ドキドキ　して　見ている。
hara hara　doki doki　shite　miteiru.

*Candidates for the entrance examination are nervously and excitedly watching for the exam results.*

心配 で 胸 が
shinpai de   mune ga

ドキドキ する。
**doki doki** suru.

*The heart beats anxiously.*

うれしくて ワクワク する。
ureshikute waku waku suru.

*Being very joyful.*

私 は ルンルン 気分 よ！
watashi wa **run run** kibun yo!

*I am in a happy mood.*

女の子　が　ニコニコ
on-nanoko ga　niko niko

笑っています。
waratteimasu.

*A girl is smiling cheerfully.*

彼女　は　全財産　を　なくして
kanojyo wa　zenzaisan o　nakushi te

オロオロ　しています。
oro oro　shiteimasu.

*She lost her whole fortune and is very upset.*

悲しみ で 心 が
kanashimi de　kokoro ga

ボロボロ に なる。
**boro boro**　　ni　naru.

*The mind is consumed with grief.*

衣服 が ボロボロ に なる。
ihuku ga  boro boro   ni   naru.

*The clothes are worn-out.*

心 が モヤモヤ している。
kokoro ga **moya moya** shiteiru.

*The mind is foggy.*

恐ろしく て **ゾクゾク** する。
osoroshiku te **zoku zoku** suru.

*Trembling with horror.*

寒く て ゾクゾク する。
samuku te **zoku zoku** suru.

*Shivering with cold.*

知らない人　が　私の顔　　　を
shiranaihito　ga　watashinokao o

ジロジロ　見た。
**jiro　jiro**　mita.

*A stranger looked intently at me.*

子供　が 動物園　で 珍しそう　に
kodomo ga dōbutsuen de mezurashisō ni

キョロキョロ　している。
**kyoro kyoro** shiteiru.

*A child looks curiously around the zoo.*

子供　は　スクスク　育つ。
kodomo wa　**suku suku**　sodatsu.

*Children grow very quickly.*

彼 は コロコロ
kare wa **koro koro**

考え を 変える。
kangae o kaeru.

*He changes his mind often.*

女の人　が 床　を
on-nanohito ga　yuka o

ゴシ ゴシ　洗っています。
**goshi goshi**　aratteimasu.

*A lady is scrubbing the floor.*

男の子　が　柿の木 を
otokonoko ga　kakinoki o

**ユサユサ**　揺さぶっています。
**yusa yusa**　yusabutteimasu.

*A boy is shaking the persimmon tree.*

主婦 が 夫の 帰りを
shuhu ga　ottono kaeri o

**イライラ** して 待っています。
**ira　ira**　shite　matteimasu.

*A housewife is irritated as she waits for her husband to come home.*

お坊さま の 頭 が
obōsama no atama ga

ツル ツル しています。
**tsuru tsuru** shiteimasu.

*A Buddhist monk's head is as bald as a cucumber.*

朝、通勤者たち　は 通勤電車　　に
asa, tsūkinshatachi wa tsūkindensha ni

**ギュウギュウ** 詰めです。
**gyū　 gyū** 　zumedesu.

*In the morning, workers are squeezed into the commuter train.*

人々　が　ヒソ　ヒソ
hitobito ga　hiso　hiso

話しています。
hanashiteimasu.

*People are whispering.*

人々　　が　　ガヤガヤ
hitobito　ga　 **gaya gaya**

話しています。
hanashiteimasu.

*People are talking loudly.*

外国人　が　日本語　を
gaikokujin ga　nihongo　o

**ペラペラ** しゃべっています。
**pera pera**　shabetteimasu.

*Foreigners are speaking Japanese fluently.*

**A brief résumé about Nobuko Ishida**
・The Associate in Arts Degree in Fine Arts （Delgado College in the USA）
・The Degee of Bachelor of Science in Mathematics(Tulane University,Newcomb College in the USA)
・Master Degree in the SHAKUHACHI （Tozanryu in Japan） Given name：Tokuzan Yamada
・Associate Degree in the KOTO （Ikutaryu, Chikushikai in Japan）
・Master Degree in the Japanese Flower arrangement(Adachishiki in Japan)
・A member of the board in Tozanryu in Japan
・Published the book titled「チョビのくれた日々」…青娥書房／"Impressive days with CHOBI"…Seiga shobō

**A brief résumé about Tamao Uchida**
・Graduated from WASEDA University in Japan
・Was a member of 漫画研究会（the club of studying cartoon） in WASEDA University
・Enjoyed becoming a cartoonist after working in an advertising company for 25 years in Japan
・Drew pictures in the following books published by「金の星社」,「あかね書房」and「青娥書房」
　　「まんが　ことわざ辞典」…金の星社／"Proverb dictionary"…Kin no Hoshi-sha
　　「まんが　きまりことば（慣用句辞典）」…金の星社／"Idiom dictionary"…Kin no Hoshi-sha
　　「子どもの権利条約辞典」…あかね書房／"Children's right treaty dictionary"…Akane shobō
　　「チョビのくれた日々」…青娥書房／"Impressive days with CHOBI"…Seiga shobō
・Has illustrated in magazines and other publications

Let's enjoy Japanese！ 日本語を楽しもう！

2016 年 8 月 20 日　第 1 刷

著　者　石田のぶ子　Nobuko Ishida
　絵　　内田玉男　Tamao Uchida
発 行 者　関根文範
発 行 所　青娥書房
　　　　　東京都千代田区神田神保町 2-10-27　〒101-0051
　　　　　Tel.03-3264-2023　fax.03-3264-2024
印刷製本　シナノ印刷

ISBN978-4-7906-0341-2 C0081
©2016　Nobuko Ishida & Tamao Uchida
Printed in Japan
＊定価は表紙に表示してあります